W9-ARG-190

Withdrawn

Scary Snakes
Cobras

Julie Fiedler

PowerKiDS
press
New York

Published in 2008 by The Rosen Publishing Group, Inc.
29 East 21st Street, New York, NY 10010

First Edition

Editor: Jennifer Way
Book Design: Julio Gil
Layout Design: Kate Laczynski
Photo Researcher: Nicole Pristash

Photo Credits: Cover, pp. 1, 9, 11, 19 (main) © Shutterstock.com; p. 5 © www.istockphoto.com/eROMAZe; p. 7 © Frischmuth/Peter Arnold, Inc.; p. 13 © www.istockphoto.com/Nico Smit; p. 15 © R. Andrew Odum/Peter Arnold, Inc.; pp. 17, 21 © SuperStock, Inc.; p. 19 (inset) © Getty Images.

Library of Congress Cataloging-in-Publication Data

Fiedler, Julie.
  Cobras / Julie Fiedler. — 1st ed.
      p. cm. — (Scary snakes)
  Includes index.
  ISBN-13: 978-1-4042-3837-4 (library binding)
  ISBN-10: 1-4042-3837-9 (library binding)
  1. Cobras—Juvenile literature. I. Title.
  QL666.O64F54 2008
  597.96'42—dc22
                                                2007007600

Manufactured in the United States of America

Contents

What Are Cobras?

Cobras belong to a family, or scientific grouping, of snakes called Elapidae. Cobras are **venomous** and some of the deadliest snakes in the world. Most people recognize cobras because they can make their neck get wide and flat right below their head. This part of a cobra is called the hood.

There are many different colors of cobras, such as black, brown, and light yellow. They can grow to be 4 to 8 feet (1–2 m) long. This book will tell you more about the world's most famous cobras.

This is an Indian cobra. It is raised off the ground and has formed its hood. A cobra makes its hood by flattening its upper ribs.

Fangs and Venom

Cobras have two short, hollow teeth, called **fangs**. The fangs are hollow so that they can **inject** venom when they bite. Venom is made in poison sacs and then flows up to the fangs. Cobras do not always inject venom when they bite, but they can be deadly when they do.

Cobra venom is a **neurotoxin**. A neurotoxin stops the body from working properly. People who get bitten can become **paralyzed**, vomit, and stop breathing. Sometimes it takes only 30 minutes to an hour for a person to die from cobra venom.

The person holding this cobra is milking its venom so that it can be used in drugs that heal bites from that type of cobra.

Where Cobras Live

Cobras live in different parts of Africa, Asia, India, and the Middle East. They live in warm places because they are **cold blooded**, which means they cannot control their own body temperature, or heat. Their main **habitats** are deserts and rain forests. Deserts are hot, sandy, and dry. Rain forests are warm, leafy, and wet.

Some cobras, such as the common cobra, live in lands used for farming rice. Cobras can sometimes even be found in towns or cities, where they will go to hunt for mice and rats.

Cobras live in hot desert habitats, like this one in Africa. *Inset:* The afternoon heat is sometimes too hot for these cold-blooded animals. This Egyptian cobra is resting in the cool space between some rocks.

How Cobras Hunt

Cobras hunt at night. They usually eat birds, frogs, mice, rats, and lizards. Some cobras even eat other snakes! Cobras will bite their **prey** and then wait for the venom to kill or paralyze it. Sometimes it takes only a few minutes for their venom to work on small animals. Cobras then swallow their prey whole.

Other animals, such as mongooses and raptors, hunt cobras. Cobras can keep themselves safe from **predators** using different **defenses**.

The mongoose has some resistance to the cobra's neurotoxins. This means that the cobra's venom does not hurt the mongoose.

Cobra Defenses

Cobras have defenses, such as camouflage, warnings, and striking. Camouflage is when an animal mixes in with its habitat to hide from predators or to surprise prey. When cobras feel **threatened**, they lift their hood and raise their body off the ground to try to scare predators. Some cobras, such as king cobras, make a hissing noise.

If those defenses do not work, cobras will strike. When they strike, cobras do not move as quickly as other snakes, such as rattlesnakes, but they can inject a lot of venom with each strike. This is one reason why cobras are deadly.

This cape cobra is in its warning position, in which it is raised off of the ground with a flattened hood. If this does not scare away the predator, the cobra will strike.

Young Cobras

Some male and female cobras use their sense of smell to find **mates**. After mating, most female cobras lay eggs, although a few kinds give birth to live young. Cobras are one of the few snakes that guard their eggs before they **hatch**. Baby cobras are 8 to 12 inches (20–30 cm) long.

As snakes grow, they shed their skin. Babies shed about 2 to 11 days after they are born. Adults shed their skin four to six times in a year. When they get their new skin, they also get new fangs, teeth, and even a tongue!

The baby cobra shown here is newly hatched from its egg. It may be little, but a baby cobra has venom that is just as strong as that of an adult!

Spitting Cobras

Some African cobras, such as black-necked cobras, are called spitting cobras. They can shoot their venom. Instead of biting, they spit the venom through the openings in their fangs. The venom comes out in two jets.

Spitting cobras aim for the eyes of their prey. Their venom causes a lot of pain. It can even cause blindness! The ringhal cobra spits venom up to 4 feet (1 m) away. There are other spitting cobras that can spit their venom up to 8 feet (2 m) away!

Although they are known for spitting their venom, spitting cobras can also give venomous bites.

Egyptian Cobras

Egyptian cobras live in the deserts of Africa and the Middle East. In Africa, they are the most common type of cobra and are often used by snake charmers. Snake charmers play music to make it look like their pet cobra is dancing and under the charmers' control. Egyptian cobras have a large head and big eyes. Their hood can be 6 to 7 inches (15–18 cm) across.

Egyptian cobras are one of the most poisonous types of cobras. They inject a lot of venom when they bite. Their strong venom kills prey quickly. They eat lizards, toads, and even other snakes. Egyptian cobras are large and quick to attack.

To keep themselves safe, some snake charmers remove the cobra's fangs or poison sacs. This causes health problems for the cobra. *Inset:* Many kinds of cobras are used by snake charmers, but the Egyptian cobra is the one most often used in the practice.

King Cobras

King cobras are the biggest venomous snake in the world. They can grow to be 18 feet (5 m) long. When they lift their body off the ground, they can get up to 6 feet (1.8 m) high. A venomous bite is strong enough to kill an elephant! They are so deadly because they can attack quickly and without warning.

King cobras live in southern Asia and can swim well. They often live near water and in rain forests. They eat mostly snakes and often eat fellow king cobras!

A full-grown king cobra is big enough that when it raises itself up, it can look a standing person in the eye. This has helped the king cobra become known as a scary snake!

Cobras and People

Cobras are deadly, but they can be helpful, too. Cobras eat animals, such as rats, that can carry germs that make people sick. Scientists also study cobra venom to see if it can be used in drugs that cure illnesses.

People can hurt cobras more than they can hurt people. When people move into areas where cobras live, cobras lose their homes. People also hunt cobras for their skin. This could lead to them becoming **endangered**.

Glossary

cold blooded (KOHLD BLUH-did) Having a body heat that changes with the surrounding heat.

defenses (dih-FENS-ez) Things a living thing does that help keep it safe.

endangered (in-DAYN-jerd) In danger of no longer living.

fangs (FANGZ) Sharp teeth that inject venom.

habitats (HA-beh-tats) The kinds of land where an animal or a plant naturally lives.

hatch (HACH) To come out of an egg.

inject (in-JEKT) To use a sharp object to force something into a body.

mates (MAYTS) Male and female animals that come together to make babies.

neurotoxin (nur-oh-TOK-sen) Poisonous matter that attacks the nerves.

paralyzed (PER-uh-lyzd) To have lost feeling or movement.

predators (PREH-duh-terz) Animals that kill other animals for food.

prey (PRAY) An animal that is hunted by another animal for food.

threatened (THREH-tund) The possibility of being hurt.

venomous (VEH-nuh-mis) Having a poisonous bite.

Index

Web Sites

Due to the changing nature of Internet links, PowerKids Press has developed an online list of Web sites related to the subject of this book. This site is updated regularly. Please use this link to access the list:

www.powerkidslinks.com/ssn/cobra/